prayer: fix my set
poems by martha boss

ISBN-13: 978-0692708408

Cover art Getty Images

Inside artwork courtesy of Martha Boss © 2016

TABLE OF CONTENTS

'when i was a child
children were seen
but not heard.
i saved a lot of what
i didn't say.
sounds from then & now
became poems.
i hope they like
being my bio.'

martha boss

I CELEBRATE

i celebrate my pen.
keeper of protest & riot.
& lately laboring
in response to
administrative sentences
phrasing sounds
like threats masquerading
as benefits with
implications & consequence.
recognized by me as
jeopardized systems
with no sleep & fluent
in schizophrenic speak.

my pen, desperate avatar
of truth, translating
crammed passion.
wishing it could wake a mighty sword,
keeping company with spirits,
early settlers,
& occupiers,
all sleeping
with one dream between them
wearing thin.
reluctant to wake
under the quilt
of ideals.

exhausted, I celebrate
my pen.
the prison of words,
doing time,
let out when
they're good & ready,
learning how to live
on paper.

THE FORCE

i love the genderless force
that may sometimes be with me.

i don't like blaming a god
for anything.
i don't like giving a god
be it a he or a she,
credit for something.

i like it when i've just thought
an amazing thought,
or done an incredible deed,
& i can say with all certainty,
the force was with me.
and if I try too hard
it's against me.
it's everywhere,
my mind at rest,

or somewhere else
& i rope it in,

or passing it on the street
then seeing it later.

it leaves
the same way
it arrives.

on sundays, with the almighty out

enmass,
the force cruises around
the pews, teasing doctrines.

the nervous faithful drink
the wine to still the something
that touched them.

i love that i can't define it.
hope for the human race
might be if the force
forever eludes
google definition.

CIVILIZATION A GREAT BEAST
HAS DEVOURED SERENITY

on the s.w corridor
early morning beats
the Acela train whistling
thru old bones.

for those long gone
this sound is a comforting
connection.

i awake with something.
my sounds.
in the morning.
quiet struggles
with new intention.
while time & time again
compete for recognition.

our inhumanness is a weapon
of mass destruction
& i am quietly at war
with my latest
proclamations.

i want funny or serious
laughter to be mine.
they flail around
in a constant sea.

i want deep sleep to purge
myself of treason.
destructive hearsay
i pick up on the walk.
Slander & wi-fi & meaningless talk.
without any notice i will
just walk out with gaps & depths
& doubt in question.

i want my manifest to be true.
long strands of inherited common
acids intertwined with a ray of
light to say my reason. i want
sounds like train whistle
declarations.

PRAYER: FIX MY SET

if I can get the tv to work
i'm hopeful all things will.
so i go straight to the Maker.

dear God,
please send me the secret
combination of green light
power box.
plus green 'on' button on set,
plus 'power' on remote,
plus 3 small red blinking
tv cable auxiliary buttons
plus 'all in' button.

 i know in the right sequence
& trips between the box,
the set & the remote,
that it will go on. as in
the past it has.
but it's always been a hit
or miss deal.
today everything misses, i don't
know. maybe it's just broken.
dear God, are you punishing
me for not believing you
created technology.
i swear i will believe
if you answer my prayer.

i will believe yr responsible
& give you credit for it
& that includes the programming.

by the way, God,
are you black or white
or some other color. red,
yellow or brown. i'm not
racist but do you also
influence the colors i've been
getting. some tones & tints
on my tv that are out-of-the-
fricking over-the-rainbow ether.
it's that or dreary shades of grey.

so.
where are you from anyway, God?
give me a sign. i'm praying.
I'm guessin' radioshack. please.
can you fix my set?

THIS MOVIE

i watched this movie with
Charlton Heston wandering
the Sinai desert.
his father, the pharaoh,
had banished him there as
punishment for freeing a
slave from certain death.

Charlton Heston, who was
Moses, believed all men
should be free, not slaves
to other men.

Yul Bryner, the Pharaoh,
was upset because his son,
Moses, didn't agree with slavery.

anyway, Moses met a shepherd girl
who gave him water &
a son & told him not to go
to the top of the mountain
because he might see God
& then she would lose him
which is pretty much what
happened.

and them Moses walked back
to Egypt where his father

was dying & Moses started
working the room & his ex-girlfriend
starts working on him & sends
his son and mother away because
she tells him the Pharaoh,
Yul Bryner, has decreed
all first-born sons to
be killed.

not unlike our military sending
the youth of today
to die on foreign soil.

it's like, they, the big guys,
don't want any competition
after they get old.

then I watched Tom Cruise
duking it out in court with
Jack Nicholson.

Tom Cruise did a good
acting job & could get
better with age when he won't
be so pretty.

the best part of this movie
was Tom Cruise having a bat.
a baseball bat that he carried
with him when he was thinking.

the bat gave him more power
over his thoughts & when
you saw him with his bat
it was true.
you could see him getting
inspired.
in this movie, too, it was
an older man giving a death
order for a younger man
who was considered a threat.

hmm. now I'm thinking
with my pen.

did God give the order
to have Jesus killed?

wasup with these guys?

TO ESCAPE

i draw every day.
every day I draw the sky.
it's usually indigo blue.
it usually gets me past
a bad memory.
if i'm lucky
sometimes it goes
somewhere carrying
my worst nightmare
faster than i can draw it.

& birds. i draw birds.
i might be in the mood
to draw a goose.
or geese doing geese things.

a comical bird.
it can do some goose thing
that says how stupid i am
if i don't laugh at it.

& that settles that
no matter how i am hurting
remembering what could finish
me off, if i don't hurry up
with the crayons coloring laughter.

i love it when a bird

stands on one leg
so the other one looks broken.
It's not really broke
& the goose knows it.
it's just being silly.

i like clouds too.
changing shape. i like to
draw a cloud turning into
something else it wasn't in
the beginning
like some nebulous metaphor.
while yr zooming down the road
in a car on a bike
& the cloud can't catch up
or it runs into a skyscraper.

sometimes when the buildings
are low the sky might be one
big wrap-around cloud.
white on a blue background
& if you look long enough

you'll see all those
not-so-silly,
suddenly very correct,
geese, taking off,
radar signaling,
doing their precise formation
dipping on command

from the head goose
showing off beside clouds.

clouds.
not sure of what they are
doing or where they're going.
just being iffy.

i draw them. & i draw geese
being precise.

i draw them honking & flapping
& dipping into my sky.
that's my flight.

SLAYING DRAGONS

like the man said
you gotta slay
your own dragons.

no point in expecting
someone else
to do it for you.

other people don't know
what yr dragons look like
& you can't describe
these many headed terrorists & their jihads.

you have to pay attention.
a dragon is always
waiting to be a dragon.

for instance,
i might go out to socialize
because i read somewhere
people are social animals.

which is debatable.
but i'll go along
with it sometimes.
& i am usually very
uncomfortable.
because i'm talking

just to socialize.
isn't that's what it means?

& after i talk i think
'boy that was awful.
i should have said
that differently'.
but i don't' really want to.

so a social scene makes me
anti-social.

but the thing is, then,
the socializing thing,
is some kind of law
it's the no-man's an-island law.

however, 2 on that island
isn't good.
after learning how to kill
each other easily & scared
it might happen to them
that's still alive,
who have learned to
like life,
some people learn
that war isn't good.

that talking is better.
so you get a lot of people

talking a lot
& that's known as
talking it out.

you have socializing
& talking it out.

whatever you call it
you can feel
all the other dragons'
differences of opinions
building up around you
& you start prepping
your dragon.

& that's when all the
other dragons come
after you & you have
to back off.
& that feels crappy
because you were having
fun. you and yr dragon
were having fun.

so there you are all by
yrself with yr dragon
out of the social circle.
& a dragon is ITS true self
when it's ostracized.

but if it's all you have
left it will threaten
to kill YOU.

so that's when
you have to SLAY IT.

HURT

hurt keeps us going.
hurt loves itself.
nourishes, feeds and medicates
its hurting self.

it will do everything in its
power to keep from getting hurt.

i thought i was alone sitting
on the couch when suddenly
hurt sat down inside me.
all smiles.
begging for company.

you can make a robot from
hard feelings.
& i know how the branches
that trusted the water felt.
when they were ice-trapped.

and i know a rock, layer
by layer, formed from what
we said & what we did when we
were hurting each other,
ourselves.

i know we owned what hurt.
i know it became a precious

stone.
i know the hold we have on
perfecting hurt until its
the diamond that cuts.

WHEN I WAS SICK

when i was sick
i learned how to be sick.

when i was a patient
i learned patience.

how to hold my breath
for a long time
waiting & counting
for long minutes.

people came around
& took vitals.
vitals tell how alive
a person is according to
the numbers that show up
in colors.

but I know differently.
i was near dead with vitals
in red & green & orange before
someone got the brilliant idea
to ask me where does it hurt.

it took them hours to get me
into the x-ray room.

they took pictures of my

breathing apparatus.
ribs and things.

that's when i lost patience
because, they told me, after all
my waiting, they couldn't
find anything.

no?
well what were you doing all
that time i was huddled &
shivering under a thin sheet
in a chair?

were you looking?
i was at least learning patience.
how to wait & how to be sick.

& i made an x-ray of me
developing myself introspectively
while i was waiting.

all it takes is for everyone
to ignore you.

THE MUSIC IN THE RAIN

the silence. in the drops.
the drowning out of soul
in the electronic ego
sound of the boom box.

the insanity of modern man
pours down in acid rain.
the mind waits outside
of the hospitals in the brain.

rain drops on the sill
fall into the rhythms
of rejoining the time
before time.
taps to the tempo remaining.
what remains of the mind.

drumming beats in the
inner ear.

everything amplified
nothing clear
but the dream
of the drug
that welcomes pain.

I DON'T CARE

i don't care how many
universes there are.
& i don't care if they're all
full of super strings
or if they are expanding or
entropic.
i just do not care.
well, ok, i care a little.
but our priorities in this
country continue to be
armies. lying down. standing.
sitting. & waiting. or mano
a mano clubbing.
we love killing.
& we are not going to improve
the situation by proving
super strings inhabit dark
matter.
first things first. ok?
let's take all that research
money & discover a new brain
as a love weapon.
something that disarms
the other guy.
what happened to the flower
children?
where are our magic shields?

going into deep space
for the answers
seems ass-backwards
not it seems we only discover
good feelings in death.

it's not that i don't like
hearing about big bangs.
i do love contemplating beginnings.
i don't love not knowing
all that explains our inhumanness.

COOKIE MAN

i'm outside.
i think i'm alone.

i have a box of fig newtons.
i break them into chunks.

the tree empties out a flock
of birds. they try out
the cookies.
they kind of peck at one & then
another & another like they're
seeing if they all taste the
same. and they're not sure
what it is.

i wasn't sure either when i
tasted them.

some fig.
but the newton cake part,—
i don't know.
all kinds of sugars. flours.
bleached & enriched.
sulfite to preserve freshness?

freshness?
when were they fresh?

it says on the box
'made in Mexico'.

hay, chica
porque y quando y como
que pasa con el Senor Newton@

i just saw the squirrel
come down the tree
& get 2 cookies.

hay chica.
esta la fantasma del
galeta-hombre.

el cookie-man esta
viviendo en el arbol
y ahora we know eso es
que pasa a los fig newtons.

OH NO

oh no
there you are again
everytime i go there

you're there
crabbing & nagging
about the scenery or something.
you don't care you just crab & nag.
i've seen the leaves drop
on yr arrival & the pigeons,
obnoxious as they are, don't
like you either.
you're always saying
they're dirty.
well so's yr trash talk
& yr face, it's creepy.
don't talk to me.
it's too hot for talk
which will heat up

if i am forced to talk
to you which is inevitable
if you invade my space
& insist with unparalleled
neediness to express your
so well-informed so-called
opinions pressed upon me
who politely responds

instead of shutting yr trap
for you,
with some comment
either unconsciously mean
or i might find another way
to let you know you're horrible.

& to spare myself unmitigated
aggravation it might just be
you just won't see me again.
i'm not sorry.
i'm glad.
i'm terrible.

HOPPING ABOUT

the birds are hopping about
on the patio.
they're eating the 100%
wheat bread.

earlier this morning
i finished off
the seeded wheat
which includes poppy seeds.

one time when i went into
the hospital
& they did the usual
piss & blood tests,

one of the things
i tested positive for
was opiates.

so they asked me
what i was using.
i said it might be the bread
i eat. it contains
poppy seeds.

oh yeah. right. they said.
& i said, yeah.
the brand name of the

bread is "When Pigs Fly".
& they said, that's not funny.

& i said, no kidding.
that's really the name.

& they said sure, sweetie,
where can we get some. ha ha.
now tell us what are
you smoking.
& i said bread.

& then they weren't smiling.
& now i realize why the store
is always out of seeded wheat.

& as for pigs flying,
yes they do.
i've seen them.

A DIFFERENT VOICE

i felt, when i gave voice
to my angry self, that i was
not myself.

but then again, i was.

the sound of an angry self
is different.
not as often,
& usually squelched.

under a rock.
put in a closet,
underground.

& the sound of it suddenly
coming up & out of all that,
frightens the instrument.

it scares itself
but it likes coming out.
& might run after you
for a while,

so it takes that while for
your quiet to show up
again.
it has to wait for that

loud angry sound
to go back under a rock.

but then when it comes out
again it's not so scary because
you found out where it lives

& if you feel like it now you
can go visit it sometimes
or take it out for a walk.
& it might be a good friend.

you never know when a loud
angry voice might be used
as a weapon on a deserving
enemy who is other than yourself
who is always squelching it.

I WALK BY THE RIVER
OF EVERYTHING

i note its progress.
usually flowing,'
it's now frozen.
it's in its laboratory
white coat.

along the reedy banks
of high bio research
i am a single digit wrapped
tight in wool from some
sheep from some other
Ireland river.

the wild winged have flown
to some place to us unknown.
we will see them again
in spring.
we will pretend the river
is the same.

in spring we will float
our boats.
the river of everything
will flow with experiment.

and the waste of ideas
have given it new data.

the river moving the mystery.
the unknowable genome
in the undertow.

CAPE DAY

when the earth shook
the Cape kept the sand
in its little locket.

i kept some sand
in my jacket.
i kept the air by
the sound of the sea.
i breathed the air
by the shore by the water.

just before the canal,
and after,
when i was fishing
& caught my grip,
i breathed deep,

troubles in, troubles out,
more innocent air,
more native ground.

when the sands settled
& i climbed the hill
to Nobska Light,

i got my fill
of feeling guided at sea
with more burden

than can be held.

when i was cluttered
& the air was pure
i breathed deep
far beyond the bridge.

a turbine of mind
still turns over that time.
when a nova is somewhere near,
i'll light the lighthouse
in a Cape daydream.
i'll keep the sand
in my jacket. a few grains.
then when the earth shakes,
& i am far from there,
to the music of a cape air,
some sand will dance
in my pockets.

BEFORE I DIE

before i die
i hope i have the courage
to write & read a terrible
rhyming poem.
when i get to wherever i'm going
i want to feel at home.

i want to solve all of life's
big problems
before i croak.

I want to leave with a clear
conscious & a clean slate
& maybe i'll die peacefully
from something i ate.

i hope its something good
like potato chips or dates.

i don't want to be in love
or in hate.
just idling in neutral
as i assess the mess.
seeing that it's all good
& it was all for good reasons
or bad
but who's to say what's supposed
to be

& how often do we get to say
'i see'.

we know when we hurt we hurt
too long
but there's so much of it
it makes us write poems
& songs
& poems & songs are right
& when life is horrible we
rhyme & hum & fly a kite
& sometimes it's so horrible
we have to laugh
& the glass is full not half
& we act dumb & give everybody
& everything thumbs up
like we're on some drug
& its happy time
& then that thing
It's running over,
that cup
because we are crazy

& the life in the egg
is in the yoke
& we have to be sad to write
something heavy,
meaningful, weighty
& mad
& not a dumb rhyme

& i hope i don't die
before my time
& i hope i get to say
'i see'
"its all been one big
joke."

THEY ARE EVERYWHERE

waiting. flocks of them, waiting
wanting a little crumb. a morsel.
a piece of something that is good.
that will promote hope, renew gratitude,
extend understanding,
restore faith.
mouths open.
hands held out. universal pleas & cries.
tell us.
say it.
say our purpose lives
and the earth with its best
expression turns with its best
face to the promises in the race
to keep itself fit for all those
who have faith it will always
be here.
& praise be to the maker of that
everlasting thing that perpetuates
the idea of prayer.
a longing for anything.
a daydream.
a memory of taste.
a hunger.
a yearning.
an imagined purchase.
it's a kind of food.
the next meal, an illusion

of being full.
flocks of all creations are
eating prayers.
continents of refugees
have become morsels
for the earth.

HERE I AM AGAIN

walking,
thinking & checking

the pond
the ducks

they're back again
loving the water

de-iced & flowing

wind blowing little waves
to bob up
& down with

or dunking down in

moving into wind
not ruffling
their feathers

its good to see
these birds
being themselves
paddling easily
in new warm weather
breezing thru water

there they are
doing their
unassuming swimming

here i am,
still walking
still thinking
of ways to escape
drowning in reflections.

PRAYER: FIX MY SET

POEMS
BY
MARTHA BOSS

www.ingramcontent.com/pod-product-compliance
Lightning Source LLC
LaVergne TN
LVHW010031070426
835508LV00005B/290